"Me? Depressed?"

A Thirty-Something Woman's Story of Depression from Disbelief to Discovery

I0103896

Beth-Sarah Panton Wright

chipmunkapublishing
the mental health publisher

Published by
Chipmunkapublishing
PO Box 6872
Brentwood
Essex CM13 1ZT
United Kingdom

http://www.chipmunkapublishing.com

Chipmunkapublishing gratefully acknowledge the support of Arts Council England.

Author Biography

Beth-Sarah Wright is originally from Jamaica, where she was born in 1973. She has traveled and studied extensively from Edinburgh, Scotland to San Juan, Puerto Rico. Dr. Wright received her Bachelor's degree, with high honors from Princeton University in Sociology and African American Studies. She received her Masters in Social anthropology from Cambridge University and her PhD in Performance Studies from New York University (NYU). She is married to the Very Rev. Robert C. Wright and they currently live in Atlanta, GA with their five children.

Beth-Sarah Panton Wright

Acknowledgements

To Chipmunkapublishing whose philosophy of de-stigmatizing mental health challenges is laudable and I believe in, thank you.

To my therapists and psychiatrists-you know who you are-thank you for your words of insight, your continued support and helping me go in the right direction.

To Zahraa, Joy, Helen and Mama Eva- Thank you! You are very special and I will not forget what you have done.

To my parents, Barbara and Keith, and my family, Andrea, Marc and Coleen, David, Melanie, Tish and Sandy, Thank you for your love, for listening, for supporting and for praying. May God continue to bless you and yours!

To my children, Jordan, Emmanuel, Selah, Noah and Moses. You remind me every day of what love is!

And to my husband, Robert. Words cannot express my deep gratitude and love for your support and love through this tumultuous journey. I love you.

Beth-Sarah Panton Wright

"Me? Depressed?"

Contents

Beth-Sarah Panton Wright

The Twelve Steps of Emotions Anonymous

1. We admitted we were powerless over our emotions that our lives had become unmanageable.
2. Came to believe that a Power greater than ourselves could restore us to sanity.
3. Made a decision to turn our will and our lives over the care of God *as we understood Him.*
4. Made a searching and fearless moral inventory of ourselves.
5. Admitted to God, to ourselves and to another human being the exact nature of our wrongs.
6. Were entirely ready to have God remove all these defects of character.
7. Humbly asked Him to remove our shortcomings.
8. Made a list of all persons we had harmed and became willing to make amends to them all.
9. Made direct amends to such people wherever possible, except when to do so would injure them or others.
10. Continued to take personal inventory and when we were wrong promptly admitted it.
11. Sought through prayer and meditation to improve our conscious contact with God *as we understood Him,* praying only for knowledge of His will for us and the power to carry that out.
12. Having had a spiritual awakening as the result of these steps, we tried to carry this message and to practice these principles in all our affairs.

The Twelve Steps and Promises reprinted for adaptation with permission of Alcoholics Anonymous World Services Inc. 1939, 1955, 1976.

The Serenity Prayer

God, Grant me the serenity
To accept the things I cannot change,
The wisdom to change the things I can,
And the wisdom to know the difference.

Beth-Sarah Panton Wright

"Me? Depressed?"

Preface

The morning I checked myself into a mental hospital[1], I left my home feeling numb and in a fog. I had kissed my children and hugged my husband good bye, knowing that something was different that day but I didn't know what. I was tired, exhausted in fact and when I kissed my family, I felt at the end of my tether. I was certainly not planning to go to a mental hospital that morning; I was actually on my way to the college where I teach. By most accounts it was a normal morning beginning with my daily commute. Except for one thing. I wanted to die. I drove very slowly with my fingers curled tightly around the steering wheel keeping it straight, because my natural instinct was to swerve the car off the road or gun it into the car in front of me. Flashes of death, invisibility, disappearance kept distracting me. I wanted to die and being behind the wheel of the car seemed like a sure way to do it.

The soft feeling of my children's cheeks was still on my lips however and as much as I felt they would be better off without me, I stopped myself from doing anything drastic. Dazed yet without incident I arrived at work, walked into my classroom and simply proclaimed to my students I would not, could not teach them that day. By that time the tears were catapulting down my face, my tongue was heavy and I began to shake. I left the building five minutes later, barely making it to my car and drove directly to the place that would become my

[1] Hereafter known as The Bridge.

13

refuge, my saviour. I needed help. I didn't know what to expect, all I wanted was to be locked away, from my husband, my children, my family, my life. The pain had to stop. I had been battling depression for about three years. But this moment, this intersection was the worst it had ever been.

It had been a harrowing few days leading up to this implosion. My work was suffering. My family was suffering. My relationship with my husband was suffering. Day to day life was so difficult it was much easier to sleep my way through. I had never felt like this before, never knew anyone who did. This was so outside of my zone of reality I didn't know what to do. So I ended up going where I was sure someone could help me to understand what I was going through and what I had to do to feel better. It was in this place, this mental institution that the idea of this book was divinely downloaded. I was staying in the halfway house at the Bridge when it became clear to me that I had to write about my experiences in order to heal and perhaps even help others.

As I checked myself in, I was a thirty-something woman, mother and wife; Christian, professional, well-educated, brought up in a safe, close, loving family environment; and I was crushing under the weight of depression. I was dying and didn't even know it. There I met other women just like me, suffocating in depression. It really doesn't matter why we were there specifically, the fact was that we were not well and we wanted to feel better. The emotions were the same. I met women there who shared their stories and I never realised just how pervasive these emotional challenges were. Story after story, so many similarities and coincidences. Black women, white women, Asian women, it didn't matter, we all had something in common and that thing was wiping us out.

When the vision of the book came to me, it was very clear. I wrote down everything word for word that came divinely downloaded into my brain. Each chapter title remains the exact same as I had scribbled it in my diary as I lay on the bed in the halfway house seeking solace and healing. Although the title of the book says this is my story, there is more here than just a story. It is about helping others in the most humble way that I can. It is about sharing what I have come to learn in the short time being diagnosed with depression and following my stint in the mental hospital. This is not a book about how I got over and am doing fine now. This is simply a moment in time, gathering all the experiences in the time leading up to this depressive episode and the time of spiritual awakening and healing afterward. It is not meant to be long or preachy or necessarily a self-help book. It is meant to be an inspiration, a motivation, some stimulation and some encouragement for other women going through similar experiences.

Although I had grown up knowing very little about depression and came from a life that one would not associate with depression, there is one thing that has helped me prepare to deal with depression. That is my faith in god. I can only sincerely thank my parents, Keith and Barbara, for teaching us as we grew, to grow in faith and the loving light of God. While I may have grown distant from God during the depths of my depression, He has been a constant throughout it all. That is why each chapter begins with a scriptural text. They set the mood and the texture of this book. And they are simply an extension of my belief system of what is woven into my body, flowing through my veins. This book wouldn't make sense without a spiritual underpinning.

I went to Jamaica, my home, for two weeks following my stay at the Bridge. I prayed and prayed about this book. I begged the Lord to help me write it and to let it be a blessing to others. I sat down for two weeks and it came pouring out. It was probably one of the best steps towards healing that I could take. The therapeutic nature of writing one's story was such a comfort during this time. Now I hand the book over to you. Perhaps you have asked yourself the same question, "Me, Depressed?" Perhaps you know someone who has. Whatever has brought you here, please take this as a humble expression of my love for you and my love for wholeness and healing. God bless you!

Chapter 1

"Aren't You Going to Take My Blood?":
Diagnosis, Disbelief and Depression

Thomas said: Unless I see the scars of the nails in his hands and put my finger on those scars and my hand in his side, I will not believe." John 20:25

  I was first diagnosed with clinical depression one rather hot afternoon in late July 2006, and hands down I was a "Doubting Thomas". I was in utter disbelief when the psychiatrist I was meeting for the first time diagnosed me as clinically depressed and as needing medication, without so much as taking out a stethoscope or a thermometer! Even writing now that I was diagnosed with depression three years ago feels odd and strange like I'm writing about someone else or as if I'm stepping outside of my skin and looking at my body and my life from the outside. This was not a part of my world of understanding. This didn't feel real.

  I sat across from this psychiatrist I had found from my insurance panel, in her modern, Target inflected, and color coordinated office in Atlanta. The beige suede couch with blue and brown cushions was necessarily comfortable and her office was just high up in the building to mute the sounds of urban life below. I sat with a wet crumpled piece of tissue in my hand, uncontrollably crying and had just started scratching the surface of my heavy thoughts when she hit me with that news.

"You are clinically depressed. You're going to need to take medication, an antidepressant, which I will prescribe for you today."

"Excuse me?" I thought. "Have I missed something?" I knew I was sad, burdensomely sad even, but this "depressed" word was really shaking me up. Medicine? I thought I was just feeling down, feeling out of sorts. Surely this would pass. I wanted to know more. How did she come up with that diagnosis so quickly? How could she tell by listening to me for such a short time? And when was she going to take my blood? Surely a blood test would confirm her speculations. After all a diagnosis is so final, so devastatingly permanent, that she couldn't have possibly concluded that without some sort of physical test, something tangible, something I could see for myself before believing her and accepting this new reality in my life.

But how did I even get to this point in the first place? I was 33 years old at the time, married for almost 10 years to a wonderful man who happens to be a priest, a mother to 5 children and a college professor. I was living my life, trying to cope with its normal vicissitudes, and simply moving forward. By many outside accounts, I had a solid marriage and a beautiful family. I had achieved academically what less than 1% of the world attain. I had attended some of the best universities in the world studying at Princeton, Cambridge and New York Universities. I grew up in a close-knit, well respected family in Jamaica with a strong faith life, and I had established my own faith journey in my adult years. Yet here I was wiping incessant snot from my nose, telling an absolute stranger about the heaviness in my life, being told I had a life threatening serious medical condition known as depression.

I emphasize these aspects of my life in order to say that depression does not discriminate. Nothing in my formal educational or professional experiences could have prepared me for the reality of depression. The prevalence of depression is unrelated to ethnicity, education, income or marital status.[2] Depression disregards it all! There seems to exist some tacit understanding that depression affects those who have grown up in adverse conditions; single-parent homes, or childhoods where abuse ran rampant. At one point I even thought that depression seemed to disproportionately affect "starving artists", musicians or incredibly talented poets. As if, depression was some sort of prerequisite for talent. In fact when I was younger and wanted so badly to be a poet I almost searched for something to be depressed about or looked to my family for something I could hold onto as "abusive" or something that affected me negatively. Well it wasn't there. I had what may be considered a picture perfect upbringing. A two parent, Christian, happy, stable household. Love abounded and we were close. I even considered my mother my best friend during my teenage years which I know is unheard of for many a teenager! Prayer was an elixir for any problem and the bible was a welcomed source of comfort. So if I had all of those things, especially a strong faith life and

---

[2] Radulovacki, Branko, "The Basics of Mental Illness" Ridgeview Institute

supportive family, why was I screaming inside? Dying slowly as each day seemed to gnaw at my soul, eroding any sense of joy or true happiness. From the outside I shone joy through my smile which people would compliment me on and even rely on. Beth would always smile and give luscious hugs, to strangers even. But with each day I was slipping away, sinking into a dark space away from my husband, my children, my family and friends. One may ask "Why do I have to battle depression?" The answer is simple. Why not you?

Despite the fact that I had a PhD and was pretty well read, I was completely ignorant about this thing called depression. Swayed and influenced by the countless images of "crazy" people on television and in movies, I did not realize that this was a serious medical condition that was more than feeling sad or down. Even if you had no "reason" to be sad, depression can creep into your life and affect nearly every aspect of it, in very debilitating ways. I had no reason to be sad. There was nothing concrete that I could point to. There was nothing in my world that I could say was making me sad. All I knew was that tears came readily to my eyes, my smile was not real and I was tired. Just simply tired.

I went home that afternoon with about 5 different brochures from the psychiatrist's office on depression, ready to share with my husband and ready to scour the internet to satisfy my newfound curiosity. I was starving for information and still grappling with the idea that I may have a mental illness. Both my husband and I had been unaware about depression in the past and as we went through the symptoms and criteria for depression in the brochures, we found ourselves saying "yeah, we all feel that…several times a day even, are we all depressed?"   So what are the criteria for depression?   According to these brochures and most literature on depression you must have five or more of the following symptoms for duration of two weeks or longer, and the symptoms are not to be found due to any effects of a substance or a medical condition.[i] The symptoms include, "feeling sad, empty, hopeless or numb; loss of interest in things you used to enjoy; irritability or anxiety, trouble making decisions, feeling guilty or worthless, thoughts of death and suicide."[ii]

I know I had felt nearly every one of those symptoms perhaps even everyday for as long as I could remember then, but did this really mean I was depressed?   That I had a mental illness?   That I needed medication, pills, to help me feel better?   I mean I had trouble deciding what to cook for dinner nearly every night.   Fatigue and I were best of friends and not a day went by recently when I felt no interest in doing what I would normally do to get out of a funk.   My three year old at the time, could tell you I was irritable for crying out loud and I chased almost every pursuit at work and at home with a shot of anxiety.   Me? Depressed?   No, it was just life.   Often when I tell other women about having five kids, a husband and a full time career, they say flabbergasted, " How do you do it?   If it were me I'd be in the Looney bin!" Little did they know that that was where I was literally heading. Little did I even know, until walking into that office on that rather hot and sticky day in late July.

Dealing with depression is no easy feat.   First and foremost it is important to know that clinical depression is a serious medical condition that affects millions of people across the world, even if they may not know they have it. Yes, it is a mental illness, an illness that affects our emotions and feelings and ways of seeing the world. It is not something that can be brushed off like having a bad day or feeling a little down. It is not something that can be cured with a swig of white rum or a night out with friends. It requires a diagnosis, a medical doctor, a psychiatrist to make this assertion. And yes it can be addressed with proper treatment and medication. Depression brings along with it, many questions, many stigmas and stereotypes. When first diagnosed with depression, it is not easy to grasp and get beyond the fact that you have a mental illness or a mental disorder. Am I crazy? What's wrong with me? Do I need to be committed? Why do I have to take medication to think and feel differently? Why can't I just be normal, like everyone else? These are just some of the questions that may arise when faced with the reality of depression. But some things you can be sure of. It doesn't feel good. The pain is unbearable.

The fatigue is ubiquitous and burdensome. You miss who you used to be or at least who you want to be. You can see the pain and disappointment and confusion in the faces of those around you. It becomes suffocating, choking out any semblance of happiness or peace or serenity. It can be debilitating.

So what do we do? Well, there is no simple answer. One of the first obstacles to overcome when facing depression is disbelief. There are too many stigmas floating around about depression.

"Me? Depressed?"

So many that they hide the truthfulness of this serious medical condition from those who may indeed need help. Too many people either do not want to believe it or do not know enough about it to recognize it in their own experiences. It is especially true of my home people, my Caribbean folk, my Jamaican sisters and brothers, where depression is rarely thought of as real. Mental illness is usually manifest in the dishevelled "madman" on the street, eating out of garbage cans and with feet so hardened by walking barefoot, they have created an inch or two of blackened flesh. Or, even here in the United States, where I have lived for over 20 years. Even though there are commercials advertising medication for depression, it still is not considered a serious medical condition by the average Joe. In fact it is rarely spoken about and there are underlying assumptions about simply "sucking it up". Just deal with whatever feelings you have and move on. In the black community, it is even worse it seems.

Depression is not even a real emotion or an accepted one. Black women especially are put in a precarious position as if they are not even allowed to feel depressed. It is the myth of the "strongblackwoman". As if those words were organically connected to each other. It is as if we women are to wear that slogan as a cape or something, always reminding us of the hardships that our foremothers and foresisters had to endure, and thereby discounting all that we may feel today. So many days I felt like screaming to the world, "I need help!" But I was silenced by these misconstrued ideas of what it meant to be depressed, or having emotional challenges. Other stereotypes of mental illness go to the other extreme, being thought of as "crazy" or schizophrenic with multiple personalities or homeless people on the streets talking to themselves. But mental illness does not have to get to this extreme before one needs help or before one is sick.

Often God tries to tell us things but we are deafened by our own thoughts or blinded from the very real signs that are there for us to see. Like the disciple Thomas, even the most obvious signs delude us. We take on the personality of the "doubting Thomas" searching for visceral evidence. Searching for evidence we can touch and smell and feel. And when it comes to mental illnesses, it is very difficult to do just that. Not only can we lose our abilities to hear and see what God is communicating but illnesses, whatever their being, can simply be thought of as an inconvenience. Especially for busy women dealing with families and/or work. Inconvenient! As if there is no good time to be sick or this illness just does not fit into the life we want to live.

Taking medication occupies too much time or is too much of a responsibility. Our well being almost becomes the last on our life totem poles. But this is where we need to begin. Believing. Being convinced. Being persuaded. Simply believing. Jesus said to Thomas, "Stop your doubting, and believe."

Diagnosis of any kind is no joke. The word itself raises all sorts of ominous feelings. There is such finality in the word and it is often accompanied by a cloud of seriousness and consequence. At the same time however a diagnosis can bring along with it a certain sense of freedom and relief. Knowing what may be going on with you brings liberation. It brings answers to the many unanswered questions you may have had and it brings a new understanding of the problem. The common saying is that knowledge is power, but in this sense it is so true for knowing empowers you to address the problem, take steps towards curing the problem, and even if there is no cure, it can give you a new perspective, an opportunity for a new way of thinking and being in the world.

Diagnosis of a mental illness like depression can be an added challenge because unfortunately there is no quick test, no litmus test of sorts to reveal what you may have. I didn't remember this at first, when I first heard my psychiatrist's diagnosis, but before going to the office, I had received in the mail, a stack of questions from the doctor's office. Questions about my energy levels, my sleep, whether or not I had still found pleasure in the things and activities I loved, my decision making process and questions of guilt and worthlessness all within the past two weeks of my life. Aha! Eureka! Here was the blood test! The litmus test! These psychiatrists didn't go to medical school for nothing! They know what they are doing and they know what they are dealing with and they know what to look for. Yes, as much as we may be clouded by our own misguidings and beliefs about depression or mental illnesses, there is a way to diagnose what is going on and treat it in appropriate ways. We just have to be able to let go of some of those beliefs.

When Thomas first heard that Jesus had risen from the dead and had revealed himself to the other disciples, he needed that practical, tangible evidence in order to believe. Like him, I was searching for something I could hold onto, for this was truly unbelievable to me. This was not what I had grown up with or seen up close. This was not something I had any real experience with. In fact in my mind depression had become a trivial accessory for the excessively wealthy with nothing else better to do. For me there was no real meaning of depression, for one could easily with sheer willpower and with prayer "shake it off" or "de-funk-ify"oneself. So logically I wanted to get my hands dirty in it, like Thomas wanted to feel the piercings on Jesus' side before accepting this unfathomable occurrence. I wanted to smell it on my hands and see it dripping off of my fingers. If I was going to be diagnosed with an illness especially a mental illness, I wanted to taste it before I was convinced that this was a part of me.

Well that's just it. It is only a part of me. Not the whole of me. I am not a depressed woman. I am a woman who has or is fighting depression. Just as if I had been diagnosed with diabetes or cancer, it would only be a part of me and not my whole existence.

One mistake I made was thinking that this was now a new definition of me and for me mental illness equalled insanity/crazy/deranged/psychotic but more insidiously, it meant weakness. And I was not weak, or so I had been telling myself for the majority of my life.

When I was 15 years old, I left my home country of Jamaica to attend school 5000 miles away in the rainy world of Edinburgh, Scotland. I ended up at an Anglican boy's school with 400 boys, and 20 girls. I was the only black girl there. Challenges blossomed into successes as I became the first black head girl of the school and made my imprint there by rallying a couple of other girls to join the army corps at school and doing the scriptural readings with a little Caribbean flair and sense of style. Yet those challenges were real and profound and many a time I found myself on the phone to my mother doubled over with homesickness and feelings of emptiness and sadness. But my coping mechanism was simple. In addition to the beleaguered long distance telephone calls, and countless nights hugging the bible my father gave to me as a going away present, I repeated to my friends and to myself my life-giving motto at the time, in a strong cockney accent, "I'm 'ard as nails, I am!" This translated into every nostalgic stereotype of black women, Caribbean women or women in general: strong, tough, can withstand all things and more, formidable, no nonsense, sensible, powerful, tallawah, a Jamaican word meaning all-powerful. I guess we all find our own ways of surviving what may seem like insurmountable odds. I was positive that I was strong despite the tears, despite the loneliness, despite the real challenges I faced while there. But I had the story of my family, of blacks, women, black women, Jamaicans; "prior colonials"/dominions on my shoulders and nothing could or would weaken me. There was no room for weakness. And sitting in that psychiatrist's office 17 years later, there was still no room for weakness. "Me, depressed? Weak?" No way!

But there comes a time to put away childish things, childish ways of thinking and being. In I Corinthians 13 Paul says "When I was a child, my speech feelings and thinking were all those of a child; now that I am an adult I have no more use for childish ways." While being 'ard as nails was one way to deal with difficulties, it was also a brilliant way to deny those difficulties only for them to resurface at a later date or in other dysfunctional ways. I had now come face to face with a moment in which I seriously had to put away this childish crutch I had been holding onto for so long. It was simply time to let it go. I was in denial about this illness and no childish motto was going to help me face it. It is no coincidence that the title of Melody Beattie's daily book of meditations for recovering addicts is entitled "The language of Letting Go". She writes that the book 'is designed to help you spend a few moments each day remembering what you know.'[3] We can transform our world into the ones we desire through the use of language, especially in this case the language of letting go. Letting go the crutches of our youth or newfound crutches in our adult years; letting go of the very negative thoughts and words we hold onto as if holding onto the one saving branch on the side of a cliff; and letting go of the insidious stereotypes of twisted ways of thinking about this thing called depression.

But it is not that easy to let go of feelings which have been simply or not so simply ingrained in our day to day thinking and which may also be confirmed everyday in the media, or in societal

---

[3] Melody Beattie, The language of Letting Go Hazelden Meditation series

expectations, especially those of mothers and wives. The message for us mothers and wives for example seems to be, "take care of everyone else, make sure they are ok, then focus on you." But often the truth of the matter is, by that time, we are too exhausted to do anything constructive or palliative for ourselves. And as a woman, wife and mother I know this to be true. What I also know is true is that this is some sort of insidious martyr syndrome and this essentially is a choice I have made. I *choose* not to take care of myself adequately instead allowing myself to suffer under the stress of it all. Letting go is about letting go of these poor choices which we allow to seep into our lives and to take over our lives like ivy on a shady back yard.

But depression does not solely affect mothers or wives. Remember depression does not discriminate! Despite the fact that depression is twice as common in women than it is in men[4], it does not change how people, either men or women, respond to the reality of a diagnosis of depression. Letting go of ingrained notions of who we are and how we see the world is equally a challenge for men and women. We have perceptions about what it means to be depressed and that can impede our recovery, our healing.

July had not only been hot in the weather but in the temperament of my home. The summer I was diagnosed our last child was turning one. And the year leading up to that day had probably been the most stressful in our lives. But I know I did not see it that way. The summer before brought many blessings: the birth of our fifth child, the advent of

---

[4] Branko Radulovacki, MD, The Basics of Mental Illness

our 16 year old nephew to live with us and my appointment as the Director of my academic program. It was indeed a year of joy and blessings but honestly, just one of those things per year would have been wonderful. All at the same time was ludicrous! Overwhelming does not begin to describe the feelings I had. But like I said, I did not see it that way. What was happening was life. Simply that. Life. And you just move forward. "'Ard as nails," I was. Ready to conquer everything that stood before me. However I began to float down that river they call "De Nile" and pushed the real feelings of tension to the background.

I have come to understand that denial is one of those comforts we seek out when faced with difficult situations. Akin to disbelief, denial is safe even protective. We don't want to see what we know to be deep in our veins. We choose to be blinded by what is affecting us at profound levels. We dismiss them as life, as part of who we are, as something we just need to go through. When realistically if they are harmful to us we don't need them at all. And no it is not *just* life. Stress. Family relations. Work. Being overwhelmed. And so many other factors that can trigger depressive episodes can be invisible to our naked unrelenting, denying eyes. Sometimes we don't even need to recognize the triggers. The effects, the resulting consequences of them can be enough to make us really open our eyes and see the truth. I was drowning and didn't even know it. I was not even reaching out for help, because I didn't know I needed it. I slowly was pulling away from my husband and my children and my family into a sea of denial and ignorance. I was numb but didn't even recognize the need to feel.

While I was in shock with the depression diagnosis, it forced me to look carefully and realistically at my life and how I was living, and what effects those choices had on my well being. After all I was in a doctor's office, with several years of tears cascading over my cheeks, in so much pain and anguish I could scarcely bear it. I could scarcely bear looking at myself in the mirror. Yes I wanted tangible evidence from my doctor, but realistically I didn't even have to look that far. I could see the evidence in the mirror, in the dark circles under my eyes. In the smile that disappeared like a fog in the mirror. In the laughing I could no longer hear. I could see the evidence in the faces of my children, especially my oldest son who would ask me "Are you OK Mommy?" Or I could see it in the anger, frustration and disappointment in my husband, who missed me even though I was in the house with him everyday. I could see it at my workplace, when I was so eager to leave as soon as I finished teaching, not wanting to talk to anyone or let them see what I was really feeling. I could see it in the classroom when I had to step out because I couldn't hold back the tears any more. But more than anything I could see it in the clenched angry fists I used to hit the pain out of me. Yes I would hit myself with such rage; my skin would swell and darken in color. I felt such disgust for myself and didn't even realise it until a doctor diagnosed me with clinical depression.

So there wasn't a physical test for depression but that did not mean there were no physical symptoms associated with depression.

One of the great stigmas connected to depression is that you can't see it, unlike seeing blood sugar levels for example in a person with diabetes. But there are physical symptoms. Symptoms like headaches, back pain, muscle aches and joint pain, chest pain, digestive problems, exhaustion and fatigue, sleeping problems, change in appetite or weight and dizziness or light-headedness.[iii] I had no idea that the eerie pain I felt in my arms and legs was not associated with exercise. In fact I had stopped exercising so there was no reason for those pains. I had felt like I had the flu, pain in my joints. I had no information about the connection between depression and pain. Depression hurts. There is no doubt about it.

Jesus told Thomas to touch his wounds and to feel for himself the piercings in his side and the holes in his hands. He then said "Stop your doubting and believe." It doesn't have to take a physical blood test or a visceral event like that of Thomas' to stop doubting and to believe. It takes reflection and a serious inventory of our lives. I would like to believe that if Thomas had stopped for a moment and recollected his experiences with Jesus, the teachings, his own travails, challenges, his own gut feelings, perhaps it would not have taken the touch of skin and woundedness for him to believe that Jesus had risen from the dead.

This is what I needed to do upon hearing my diagnosis. Take the time to do an honest inventory of my life to look deep within and to recognize the truths in my life. It had gotten to the point for me where my emotions, my challenges, my now new depression had taken over and my life was rendered unmanageable. I needed help and I can honestly thank God now for pointing me in the direction of a psychiatrist with whom I could learn from and more importantly trust with her expertise.

Depression is real. It is not something that can be shaken off with a few pep words and a can do attitude. It is a serious medical condition that affects millions. Currently antidepressants are the most prescribed drugs in America. 25 percent of adults will have a major depressive episode at some point in their life. According to Dr. Kelly Posner, an assistant professor at Columbia University College of Physicians and Surgeons in New York City, depression is a major public health issue. Basically, it doesn't matter where you come from, or what you have achieved in life, depression can become a part of you life and can affect those around you who love you. Depression is not something to be embarrassed about. The fact is depression and other mental illnesses still remain the butt of many jokes on television and even though there are commercials now advertising the medications for depression, people still are ignorant about the reality of it and the severity of it.

I was embarrassed by the thought of having a mental illness, and even more disturbed by the thought that I was weak and could not handle what other people have handled and continue to handle every day. However if I continued thinking that way, I would not have gotten the help I needed. Depression is not a sign of weakness or failure. We would never say someone who has cancer is weak. Depression is an illness caused by chemical imbalances in the brain. But knowing the cause of depression does not necessarily make it any more real. The pain makes it real. The anguish makes it real. The tears make it real. The loneliness makes it real. The distress makes it real. The self-hate makes it real. The lack of control makes it real. The physical discomfort makes it real. The sleepless nights makes it real. The sleeping too much makes it real. The sadness and longing in the eyes of those around you makes it real. Look within. Stop your doubting and believe.

Chapter 2

"What About Prayer or Willpower?":
Medication and Depression

"In times of trouble I pray to the Lord; all night long I lift my hands in prayer but I cannot feel comfort."
Psalm 77:2

That auspicious day in July was only the beginning of my journey towards discovery in depression. It took two other diagnoses by two other psychiatrists before I truly began to become reflective and introspective and begin the journey towards healing. Yes I had a second and a third opinion over a course of two years before accepting I had a mental illness known as depression. I was not getting better. The sadness was still suffocating, yet the stigmas and questions were still abounding preventing me from getting the help I needed. Having to take medication to address my depression was a whole other story in and of itself! Medication? To cure my feelings? It just didn't seem to make sense to me. What about prayer or willpower to get me out of my funk? Having a rather strong faith life, I relied on prayer and will to heal. I could pray for forgiveness for hurting my family or myself. I could pray for peace in my soul. I could literally will myself back to health.

However, what I didn't count on was the unfathomable, that I couldn't pray, or did not know what to pray for to gain any comfort. There are times, like the psalmist above proclaims where prayer does not elicit the comfort and solace one searches for. Or at least it seems that way. While I was in the mental hospital I met a woman who, with depression and an addiction, was so ashamed to tell me or her prayer warrior mother that she could not find it in her during her worst pain to pray. She was so ashamed, embarrassed to share with her mother that she could not pray. I thought, thank God, I am not alone. Prayer sometimes eludes the tongue. I have felt that I was not worthy enough for God to take care of me. Or that my problems were not really problems. In church, I would feel repulsed at taking communion, for I felt my body was too disgusting to invite that sacredness in. But no matter, I have found that prayer remains an integral part of my medication for depression.

I thought of naming this chapter "The seven P's of medication" of which one is prayer. But prayer alone is insufficient medicine for depression. The other P's are different forms of medication I have found now to be essential on my journey towards healing. They are Prescription Medicine, Prayer, Positive Self-thinking, Playing, People, Psychiatrists and Psychotherapy.

Prescription Medication

After I was first diagnosed and given a prescription for an antidepressant I was hesitant to take it. But I was feeling pretty awful and needed to try something anything to get better. So on the day I first took the medication I was expecting to feel a major shift in my mood or some form of tingling or an explosion in my body to totally disrupt the heavy feelings of sadness and pain. I prepared myself for this major jolt and downed the pill with a glass of water. I waited and waited. What did I feel? Nothing. Absolutely nothing. Was it working? Was it the right dosage? Where was the dramatic change?

Then I looked again at the bottle, "Takes effect in 4-6 weeks." No way! Not being totally convinced about my depression, plus having to take medication for such a long time to feel an effect was not appealing in the least. But I was desperate for some change so I continued for a while. A day turned into a week and a week into a month. Then I was fine. Just fine. I was feeling like myself again and I attributed it to the medication and time, then I did what I learned I should never do, I stopped taking it. After all everything was back to normal. Well at least I wasn't crying all the time or feeling sad or anxious.

The sun was shining, and being a daughter of Jamaica, I do love the sun. The kids were out of school and my husband and I took the family on a road trip. What more could I ask for? I certainly did not need any more medication, things were just fine. I even stopped going to my psychiatrist because at this point "I got it!" I was in control once again and I was moving forward with a smile, to boot. I came to rely on my own strength once again, 'ard as nails!

Then I felt it. The slight dizziness. The strange headaches. The feeling that my brain was loose in my skull. My body was in withdrawal from the medication! I stopped without consulting my doctor or anything. I just stopped taking the pills. At first it was the physical ramifications of not taking the medication anymore. Then I found I was getting overwhelmed too quickly, agitated and irritable, before long I was back in a Psychologist's office seeking help. Well it turns out that one of the main reasons for a nonresponsive treatment for those with depression is non-compliance, or not taking the medication!!! Fifty percent of African-Americans who have depression don't seek treatment for it according to Dr. Posner. "Not enough people are getting the treatment they need." she concluded. While an adequate trial period for a prescribed medication is 4-6 weeks, a longer trial increases the likelihood of response or return to functioning.[iv] It is imperative to keep taking the medicine, to give it time, to give it a chance to work with your body. After all, it may not be the right fit. There are other reasons for nonresponse such as undertreatment in dosage or duration, a misdiagnosis, physical illness or a personality disorder.[v] These are to be discussed with your doctor, but I do know that not taking the medicine because you feel great after a relatively insufficient amount of time, just won't work!

Psychotherapy

Whereas prayer and prescription medicine are staples, psychotherapy is the soup in which they flavour. Apparently a combination of medicine and psychotherapy is most effective for treating major depression.[vi] And even in cases of mild to moderate depressive episodes, psychotherapy is instrumental in the process towards healing. Psychotherapy is officially defined as the treatment of mental disorders by counselling and psychoanalysis, etc.[vii] I see psychotherapy as an opportunity to talk in a safe environment, with someone whose professional expertise guarantees confidentiality. It's a time to be unafraid because this person hopefully has your healing in interest and wants to help. I talk a lot about feeling safe and unafraid because I fear talking to people! I am also a performer and a professor used to standing in front of a classroom filled with students or an audience, so this may sound strange. Put me in front of a large group and I am fine. Put me at a dinner table with friends and I am petrified. I am petrified to speak.

I grow huge knots in my throat, my hands shake and I feel nauseated. I am so nervous that my mouth becomes dry and I can barely squeeze a word out. I could go the whole evening without saying a word. But smiling, always smiling. We wear the mask. Because of my social anxiety, one would think I would be reticent to share with a psychotherapist. However I have learned that I share quite freely primarily because I fundamentally trust the psychotherapist. I trust him or her not to judge me, not to laugh at me or think I am weak. I trust them because they know what I am going through and most importantly they can teach me the necessary tools to go forward.

I try to be as honest as possible reaching deep within to elicit any feelings that may have been buried down there. I talk about my younger years, growing up in Jamaica, in my family. And trust me, every family has their issues no matter how idealistic they may seem. Family of origin issues follow you throughout your life. Into your relationships, your friendships, your marriage, the way you raise your children, even into your politics for crying out loud! But this is not about blame.

No, this is not an opportunity to focus on other people and what they may or may not have done to impact your life as you know it. It is about forgiveness and letting go, and letting God take over. And about understanding for yourself who you are and why you make the decisions you do, and if those are even wise decisions in the first place. Even though I had not been diagnosed with clinical depression until recently, I had visited professional therapists before. Not for any long period of time but to help when going through a particular issue, especially identity issues when I was in Scotland. Here I'm speaking primarily about school counsellors and guidance counsellors. But as an adult, a grown woman with a husband and children and a fairly strong faith life, I did not think even think about going to see someone in this capacity for help.

How did a psychiatrist even come into my radar screen? Because a psychiatrist certainly wasn't there initially. Psychiatrists were for people with "real" problems. Psychiatrists were certainly not for me who really didn't have any problems. Willpower, prayer, inner strength. They were what were guiding me, unfortunately, into some eternal abyss of depression. They were all I needed to get through on my own, so I thought.

I know an angel. This angel happens to be squeezed into the body of an 86 year old beautiful woman, who helped me to realise that willpower, prayer and inner strength was not enough to get through my depression. It was to her on the porch of her daughter's house, that I admitted that I could not go on without something different. I was powerless. The emotions of fear, sadness, anguish, fatigue, frustration had taken over and I could not see a way out. Perhaps the timing was slightly out of sequence, but if I hadn't shared with someone I trusted the nature of my thoughts, I would still be swirling down the vortex of depression, without finding a way out. It was then she suggested getting help. Help from someone who had more experience with matters such as these. The word depression never really came up in our conversations, but how could it? These were matters beyond both our areas of knowledge. But I thank God for sending me this angel and putting me in the right direction. Mama Eva, I thank you, I thank you, I thank you.

Seeing a psychotherapist for me is about learning to change my behaviour, my patterns of thinking which in truth are destructive. My most challenging behavioural change has been to adopt positive self-thought, that is making the choice to say something positive to myself rather than my more familiar tearing down myself. Tearing myself down I now know is a choice I make. I must get some sick satisfaction from it. Seldom was the time I was kind to myself. I tore down myself both mentally and physically for years. But it was such a part of me, I didn't see its negative consequences. After some time in psychotherapy however, I have come to understand that that is an extension of the low self-esteem I felt and again I gained some sort of sick satisfaction from it. Or else I would have stopped. Positive self thinking has become the punching bag for my fists. And they hurt when they touch these positive self thoughts! They protect me from my fists and the plethora of negative self thoughts which infiltrate my mental space on a daily basis.

When I do something, perhaps host a dinner for my husband's work colleagues, for the most part the dinner would go lovely but maybe one thing did not turn out as well as I had hoped. Like the time I cooked steak and I was such in a hurry not to burn the steak that the steak came out rather pink. Well I was embarrassed but managed to fix it and everyone was happy. But 10 years later I still remember that moment and these intrusive bullying thoughts come bulldozing through my head and tell me "you're a failure", "You can't even make steak!" And I get angry with myself and those who may have judged me (even though they did not). Positive self-thought, is controlling those disturbing words, stopping them and making the choice to say something more constructive and confidence boosting. Like, "I put the undercooked meat back in the oven and everything was fine, and everyone was happy." "The dinner was beautiful, we had a little adventure with the meat but the dinner was lovely." Or "I made a lovely meal, with a few adjustments, it was just delicious." Positive self-thought should really be the seventh P of medication, especially for me for those sporadic negative thoughts that infiltrate my mental space, happen too frequently and eat away at my self-esteem and self-confidence. I need to ban them from my head and the only way is to spray them with the more powerful positive self-thoughts I consciously and deliberately have to utilize.

Psychiatrists

Psychotherapy is an integral part of healing depression, but psychotherapy does not have to necessarily take place with a psychiatrist. Professional counsellors, therapists, psychologists also do psychotherapy. In fact I only recently learned that more and more psychiatrists are doing less therapy and more medication management. This is why psychiatrists must be a part of your healing especially if you are on medication. They are the ones who know what to prescribe, how much and what interacts well or not so well with what. Sometimes a particular drug may not work and others need to be tried, and it is the psychiatrist who manages the medication. Psychologists, professional therapists etc can't.

And I did what I later was told was not a good idea. I had my primary care physician instead of a psychiatrist prescribe my medicine. Easy? Sure! That's why I did it. I was seeing a psychologist and getting my medication from my general physician, but neither could see that I needed a change in dosage and that's when I headed towards the mental institution. Perhaps seeing a psychiatrist, in fact I am pretty sure, that seeing a psychiatrist would have influenced my checking into that mental hospital. Psychiatrists are the medication managers and we need them! Now I have a consistent psychiatrist. Our meetings don't last longer than a few minutes, in which he asks me how I am doing. How I am sleeping, eating, etc. I have found that I get drowsy taking the medication, but he has a remedy for that. He knows what drugs can energize me and which ones make me drowsy. He tells me when to take them as taking them at night for example logically is the best time to accommodate for the drowsiness. I have also found that I have put on a lot of weight with the drugs, as this is one of the side effects. It is more difficult to lose this weight while taking these drugs but I'd rather have the few extra pounds than a lifetime dealing with the devastating effects of depression.

Prayer

When I was a child I would have nightmares, strangely enough nightmares about being tickled. Well they were awful to me and sometimes I would wake up in a fright. My father a minister himself, on one of those fright-filled nights taught me to open up my bible beside my bed to psalm 27. "The Lord is my light and salvation, whom shall I fear? The Lord is the strength of my life, of whom shall I be afraid?" Since then I have held onto that psalm as a weapon against anything that should scare me from exams to difficult conversations, to breaking up with boyfriends. So prayer was not an unfamiliar concept to me. In fact prayer interrupts my day quite frequently and sporadically. So you can only imagine the foreign nature of not being able to pray when I was in the depths of my depression.

During those times when I could see no way out, when the tears flowed so readily down my cheeks, when I was choking in my sadness, I barely had breath to pray. I barely had breath to pray. I felt unworthy to even pray. And the shame that consumed me was suffocating.

"Me? Depressed?"

I did not get angry with God, but like the psalmist, I could find no peace, no answer, and no consolation in prayer and so like my medicine, I stopped praying. But it was in this time of silence that I heard, like a scream torpedoing through the air, an elixir through the voice of my angel on earth, Mama Eva. At a breakfast I had for women in my church on Holy Saturday, I asked her to speak to us and she shared what I have planted into my subconscious: "In the same way the Spirit also comes to help us, weak as we are. For we do not know how we ought to pray; the Spirit himself pleads with God for us in groans that words cannot express." (Romans 8:26). In other words, when prayer does elude us, and sometimes it truly does and we do not know what to pray for or even have breath to pray, the Spirit will intercede and pray for us through groans and moans, and gut wrenching sounds that words cannot express.

In the same way I came to rest in the assurance that someone else was praying for me. My mother is a prayer warrior even though she may not describe herself as such. But she talks to God like she talks to a friend. There are four of us siblings, and depending on what life brings us, she puts us in order on her prayer list. From divorce, to financial troubles, to grandchildren's sickness, she prays and prays. Knowing this when my tongue is too heavy with pain to pray, strengthens me. I simply ask. Please pray for me. And I know that she will and that will be enough. Sometimes I simply do not have the energy, the desire, the strength to pray, but I believe that someone is praying for me. Maybe even a total stranger.

Even if you are not familiar with prayer, and you are wallowing in a river of anguish it may be helpful to know that churches all over the world, individuals all over the world are praying for you. They may not know you by name but you are being prayed for. In my church tradition, the Episcopal Church, we have a Book of Common Prayer. There are many prayers that reach out anonymously to those who are suffering in body or in mind, but I have one which is my favourite: Keep watch dear Lord, with those who work, or watch or weep this night, and give your angels charge over those who sleep. Tend the sick, Lord Christ; give rest to the weary, bless the dying, soothe the suffering, pity the afflicted, shield the joyous, and all for your love's sake.[viii]

Or, from the Anglican tradition of prayers, which is used around the world: Hear us, o Lord, as we remember before thee those who have special need of thee at this time; those who are handicapped in the race of life through no fault of their own; those who have lost the health and strength that once were theirs; all who lie in pain; the blind, the deaf, the dumb; the hungry and the homeless; all refugees and displaced persons; those who are in doubt or anguish of soul, and all who have wandered away from thee. Succour them, O Lord and raise up helpers for them in need, for the sake of Jesus Christ our Saviour.[ix]

When I was in the mental hospital we had to attend a variety of group therapies and lectures and talks. One group that I attended, which I had never heard of before is called Emotions Anonymous. I had heard of alcoholics anonymous before, primarily from TV: "Hi my name is ***** and I am an alcoholic. Hi *****" I didn't know there was such a thing for people suffering from mental or mood disorders. When I was introduced to the Twelve Steps of Emotions Anonymous, I was so pleasantly surprised to see the reliance and surrender to a higher Power as we understood him. I was even more relieved to see the eleventh step: Sought through prayer and meditation to improve our conscious contact with God as we understood Him, praying only for knowledge of His will for us and the power to carry that out. What I thought I had lost, the ability and even desire to pray was now an integral part of my journey towards healing and wholeness. I believe it is no accident that the Twelve step tradition from alcoholics anonymous to emotions anonymous to co-dependents anonymous all have as their root base surrender to a higher power and use of prayer. I have included the Twelve Steps at the beginning of this book and will speak more about them towards the end. However, as I spoke with others who attended the Emotions Anonymous meetings, I learned just what hard work is entailed in following those steps. For many, the first step is such an obstacle to surmount. It simply states that we admit that we are powerless over our emotions and that our lives have become unmanageable. It doesn't seem that difficult yet to actually mouth those words is an unbelievable feat. It took me two to three years, truthfully more like 10 -12 years to admit that I was in pain, and that pain was taking over my existence. Sometimes it takes until you are drowning before you can scream out for help.

I have to thank God for these dark times, these challenging times. I was struck by another prayer, the United Thank Offering prayer which says: "Keep us ever thankful for all the blessings of joy and challenge that come our way." Our challenges are blessings too, for it is in these times that we grow, we learn, we walk closer to God, even if we are angry with him, we still have that connection to him. It is in these times that we can recognize that we are not alone, because the spirit will intercede, complete strangers are praying for us, and God finds a way, some way to bring healing and wholeness into our lives. After all it was within the walls of a mental hospital, when I was at my lowest that I discovered the Twelve Steps of Emotions Anonymous. How ironic is that?

People

How can people be medicine, especially when at times, it is other people who may be causing your pain? I know I may not have a history of abuse, but I do recognize that many depressive episodes have at their root an abusive history with other people involved. Knowing this in addition to my touch of social anxiety, it is somewhat ironic for me to be pushing people as a form of medicine. Many a time I would simply prefer to be alone. But as a woman I met in The Bridge said to me with such insight, "community takes the "c" out of crazy."

I met this beautiful woman in the halls of The Bridge where there was already a community of likeness, of people who could understand what I was going through because they were also going through it and more. She explained that having this community of people around makes you feel less "crazy", less alone, less different. For me, I found it liberating. Freedom! Mental emancipation! I could be and feel and think and speak freely because I felt I would not be judged. But what about outside those walls; family, friends, colleagues who are not as privy to the unpredictability and familiarity of mental illness?

After I had been hospitalized I found myself face to face with people's questions and queries about how I was feeling. How much do I say? I asked myself. Should I tell them everything? Can I trust this person with this information? I can't say who to trust and who not to, or who to choose to be friends and who not to, but I can say that the one constant in all of this is me. I had to be true to myself. So I would take risks and with unabashed confidence (even if I was only pretending) I would say "I have been battling depression." Like I would say I have been fighting diabetes, or I have been fighting cancer if I had them. It is an illness and millions of people around the world have it. Chances are if the person you are talking to doesn't know someone who has depression or has had experience first hand, it always is a teachable moment, an opportunity to pull back the veil of ignorance which has covered this very real, very serious illness.

While writing this book I was faced with similar situations. I would say for example, I am writing a book, and that be all. Often that would be enough information however, sometimes people wanted to know what I was writing about. One morning while I was in Jamaica recuperating and working on the book, I went walking that morning and met a woman, Julie, who became my walking partner for that day. We got along well and shared the basic information about each other. It turned out she was the director of a spa and a few days later my sister-in-law and I went for a "day at the spa" for her birthday. We had a wonderful time by the way and Julie and I were talking and I told her I was in Jamaica writing a book.

"What's the book about?" she queried eagerly.

"Well, it's a memoir of sorts about battling depression. I have been battling it for some time now…the book is called….." And I told her the title.

"Really?" she replied with surprise. I wasn't sure what next I would get but what I got was so refreshingly honest and real. And I loved her for it. She said, "I would love to know more…I think I've been depressed but haven't done anything to address it…I've been embarrassed," she whispered, "And I haven't had much experience with this at all."

It was a moment of liberation. I needn't be afraid or embarrassed. This was therapeutic for her too. Being honest with others, but more importantly with me contributes significantly on this sojourn into healing.

Just take the risk sometimes. Only you know. Trust yourself. Trust your gut instinct. People can be therapeutic. Being alone or pulling away through secrecy, or fear of being judged, will only foster alienation and discontent. People can do a world of good!

Playing

In a group therapy session I heard a psychiatrist say that for thirty years he has been prescribing a medication that his patients continually refuse to fill. The medication is exercise, or what I like to call play. Exercise is by far the cheapest medication you can get that actually helps depression. In fact according to the four tools of recovery established by The Bridge, proper eating/nutrition and exercise are one. The others by the way are medication management, psychotherapy, and support groups, like Emotions Anonymous.

It is baffling that exercise is one of the most difficult prescriptions to fill, but it is completely understandable. It takes a lot more effort to go outside and take a walk than popping a pill in my mouth. But, oh that wonderful but! Exercise works! It raises levels of serotonin, the feel good hormone and it has countless benefits for the body separate and apart from depression. Yet the excuses we come up with are many.

While I was checked in at the mental hospital I found it fascinating that exercise, or gym was mandatory everyday except for one. It was built into the whole healing system. Yet when we would go to the gym, many of the patients would sit around and use this opportunity to chat and hang out. Once again reneging on a medication.

I like to refer to exercise as play because the children in us all like to play. If I tell my children to go outside to get some exercise, they moan and groan and would rather sit on a couch watching Hannah Montana. Yet if their friends come over and say lets go play, they are gone in an instant. I love to dance so I make sure whenever I am going to the gym or going for a walk in my neighbourhood, I have my iPod with all my favourite songs. And I dance while I walk, I sing and may look a little unusual, but I am having fun!!!

So it's playing to me not exercise and I have come a long way in understanding that "playing" is like taking medication. If I miss it that day, then I can feel the effects of missing my medication. When I forget to take my prescription medication, and I have done that, I can truly feel the effects. I may become more irritable, my mood may change, physically, I may feel dizzy. It has come to be the same way with "playing". If I don't play, I may be in disarray all day!

But this is not to say that I consistently "play". I must admit that I think about it every day even if I don't actually get out and do it. I wish sometimes I would go everyday but I don't. Some days are better than others. Some days I have energy to do the things I need to do, some days I do not. Some days I have more of a desire to do the things I must do and other days I do not. I have come to understand that this illness brings along with it, good and bad days. Some days are simply better than others. And I am learning how to be at peace with that.

Chapter 3

"I Can't Take It Anymore!":
Suicide and Depression

The sorrow in my heart is so great that it almost crushes me…Take this cup of suffering from me!"
Matthew: 26:38-39

Suicide is not an option. Even though it may seem like the one that makes most sense, as distorted as that is, there is always a better option. Suicide is simply not an option if you are feeling depressed.

I wanted to write about suicide in this book because it is real and because having suicidal thoughts is one of the primary criteria for depression. For many in the depths of depression, it is a very real and even practical option. An option that for some reason seems to be the best or only one. Writing about suicide is not about planting a seed in the minds of those depressed or at their wits end; and it is not about fostering a seed that may already be planted. This chapter is about ripping that seed from the ground and not giving it any sunshine or water so it will wither away and eventually disappear. Suicide is not an option.

For many years, suicide was certainly not an option for me. In fact, the concept was an elusive one, a tragically romantic one for artists, and lovers in Europe. It seemed so far away from my sphere of reality.

But depression, this disease is an insidious one that creeps into your soul, your mind, your body, feeds on insecurities and fears, and twists your thoughts into a web of disillusion, anger and despair.

Did I have suicidal thoughts? Yes. Did I want to kill myself so that everyone, my children, my husband would be happier? Yes. Depression distorts your rational thinking. I was convinced that the world, my babies, my husband would be happier if I were not around for good.

My thoughts did not begin as suicidal ones. They were more about self-harm, punishing myself for my behaviour for my actions, for my failures. As I shared earlier I started to hit myself about 11 years ago when I first got married. The first two weeks of marriage for me were incredibly difficult. They were difficult because I had been naïve and sheltered into thinking that love would conquer all, including the dirty laundry and the vicissitudes of daily living with another. Love does not conquer all, and where other successes and achievements came relatively easy to me, this was kicking me in my behind. Marriage was a mountain I could not seem to climb over. It would continue to grow each time I made a few steps up the incline. What was making me angry, and I realise now it was anger more than anything, was my inability or my choice not to deal with the challenges head on. Not to communicate effectively with my husband. Not to be honest and forgiving to myself.

At this point it is unclear to me what precipitated the first self-harming episode, but I can clearly remember the pounding I took as a result of it. I would never hit myself in front of my husband. Instead I would go into the bathroom or another room alone and clench my fists. While screaming at the top of my lungs, I would punch myself in the face, across the very same cheeks that were once caressed by loving hands. I would hit my thighs with such force, they would swell. And I would scream with such vigour that I could taste blood in my throat and my heaving chest would ache. In some perverted way I would feel relief. Solace. Even peace.

This continued throughout my marriage and throughout my pregnancies. My actions throughout my pregnancies were particularly disturbing to me. Finding out I was pregnant was and continues to be the most glorious time in my life. Each pregnancy brought such immense joy. But at that point I knew nothing of the possibility that I was depressed, or that depression could do this to me.

I do remember lying on the bathroom floor, my cocoa-buttered belly protruding from under my nightgown, and me writhing in emotional pain. And yes I hit myself but created a vicious cycle. Because the more I hit myself, the more I begged forgiveness from my unborn child; the more I felt like a failure for doing this with this precious being inside of me. Today, I may see one of my children get frustrated and bang his head against the wall. What may be a "normal" childhood response, becomes a direct result of my violent episodes in my mind's eye. I think he must have inherited it from me and I feel so guilty for passing on such a destructive behaviour. I try to teach him and all my children that outbursts are not the most productive response to frustration. I only wish I could teach myself that. But the rage is just under the surface, and uncontrollably erupts. Self harm is best understood as the intentional, direct injuring of body tissue without suicidal intent. Although the primary intention of self-harm is not to commit suicide, they are related.

As the time went on, the mountain continued to grow and I could barely make any headway. Before long my thoughts of self-harm transpired into suicidal thoughts. Thoughts of simply ending it all, so I wouldn't have to tackle that mountain anymore, and that those around me would not have to see their mother, their wife failing miserably each and every day. I felt I could no longer take it anymore!

When I consider Jesus' words in the garden of Gethsemane, the day he would be betrayed and arrested, I hear my own words and feelings: "*The sorrow in my heart is so great that it almost crushes me…Take this cup of suffering from me!*" Yes, indeed take this cup of suffering from me! Take this failure to climb this mountain away! To know that Jesus himself felt this weakness of the flesh, this utter despair and anguish consoles me. Following his thoughts, and knowing his impending suffering and death, it is not unfathomable that he may have considered suicide. Considered ending it before it all transpired. But Jesus does something which the eleventh Step of Emotions Anonymous compels us to do, he prays for God's will to be done. "My Father, if this cup of suffering cannot be taken away unless I drink it, your will be done." (Matthew 26:42) Moreover, the eleventh Step also says to "pray only for knowledge of His will for us and *the power to carry that out.*" It certainly is not easy, but praying for the power to pull through, to face the suffering, to climb the mountain; all rejects that idea of suicide, of ending it prematurely. Suicide is not an option.

In The Bridge, I met numerous friends who had considered suicide, who had held the pills in their hands, who had sliced their wrists with a razor blade, who had a noose waiting in their car. But I thank God that life succeeded. Because I met life-giving nurses, sensitive and gifted poets, astute businessmen, animal loving veterinary students, shrewd legal minds, invigorating stay at home moms, empathetic therapists and brilliant beautiful women in the prime of their lives. I do not know what God's will is for me or for any of us, but I do know that according to the bible, the Lord says, "I alone know the plans I have for you, plans to bring you prosperity and not disaster plans to bring about the future you hope for." Jeremiah 29:11. The Lord wants us to be joyful, to be hopeful and like the Twelve Steps we can ask Him for help. He can "restore us to sanity", we are to humbly ask him to "remove our shortcomings" and we are to be "entirely ready to have Him remove all these defects of character." We are valuable. Seeking help through a diagnosis, with psychotherapy and playing we prove to ourselves that we are worth it all. Suicide is not an option.

When I found out that it is more likely that my children were to commit suicide if I did, I just couldn't bear it. To think of the pain I would cause them, the unanswered questions, the guilt, the blame, the self-doubt, the utter shame of it all, I just feel like I could never do that to my children. But honestly I feel trapped in this world because of those feelings. I feel damned if I do and damned if I don't. It is such an awful thing to write, to actually mouth my lips around these words. But it is being brutally honest. Logically I know that God has plans for my life, but the despair I feel in this life couldn't be what He has in store for me. Or perhaps it is for a season. As I said before I do consider these trying times as blessings because they help to strengthen certain emotional muscles and they somehow bring you closer to God, and to knowing yourself. But the pain ekes away at my existence and my soul is left emaciated. The suicidal thoughts come flooding in. It is not as if I choose to have them. I don't intentionally sit down to conjure ideas about suicide. They are almost gut reactions, automatic solutions to the anguish I feel. It is a twisted and unhealthy thing to think that the world would be better off without you in it. But it is a very real emotion and truthfully, it is oftentimes considered as the only option.

I told someone close to me that it seemed so much easier to turn on the car in the garage and simply go to sleep to never wake up. He told me in response that suicide is such a cowardly thing to do. Instead of sticking around and facing the problems and even attempting to change them, it is a coward who chooses death and disappearance. I didn't know how to take that. In fact I felt angry, disgruntled with the fact that if I were to kill myself, the lasting thought would be that she was a coward. A coward? Great. It is as if I lived in failure and would die a failure. I still don't know how to understand that comment. What I have come to understand that it is difficult to face the hurt and the causes of depression. It does take an incredible amount of emotional fortitude to draw out the grief, to revisit sensitive terrain and make sense of it all. Cowardice doesn't always mean weakness. It can also mean fearfulness. To think I am too afraid to stay and deal with my issues, is more palatable. Depression after all is fear and anger turned inwards. But there is help available when it comes to fear. The seven P's of medication comes in useful here again. Psychotherapy is there to guide you through fear. People are there to hold your hand while you face fear. Playing and exercise can help to alleviate fear. And prescriptive medication is there to help you to control fear. Suicide is simply not an option and it is not the answer to fear.

When those images of suicide resurface, when I think they would be better off without me, I think of my children. I see their precious faces and I don't want them to feel any of what I feel. Perhaps you don't have children, or feel like you have no one to turn to, but you do. The world needs you. Needs your experiences. Needs your wisdom, and you do have wisdom. With every new day, you gain wisdom. The world needs your gifts, and you do have them. The world needs your being and presence. Suicide is not an option.

Chapter 4

"A Mental Hospital? But I'm Not Crazy! ":
Getting help and Depression

"Why are you standing out here? I have a room ready for you in my house…" Genesis 24:31

Two weeks before I checked myself into The Bridge, I had a rage episode. I felt out of control. I literally did not have power over what was coming out of my mouth or my physical actions. My voice was enraged. I felt it rising inside me like an active volcano on the verge of eruption. I was agitated and irritated. I grabbed my husband with frustrated hands. In the proximity of my children I raised my voice. I stormed up the stairs screaming. The next moment I was writhing on the floor in my closet hysterically. I was alone. And the anguish I was feeling was unbearable. I hadn't had an episode like that in a while. As I reflect now on my experiences I realise that my anger explodes when I feel I have no control. In a distorted way, the only way I gain control is to scream and hurt myself. As I described in the chapter before, self-harm is my primary way of gaining control, and the fear and lack of control I feel converges into a hot abyss in my broken soul and just erupts with much consequence. Before, it was only my husband who experienced these outbursts by me but with this episode my children heard. It must have scared them to death. It was a transformative moment for me. Because now my children saw me in a new light and I was forever different to them.

Five days later continuing this maniacal rage, I found myself in my car, screaming hysterically, my chest heaving like I had been running for miles. Each scream ripped away at the lining in my throat and I held on to the steering wheel so tightly that my knuckles were white. I didn't know where I was driving to, I had no real destination. I just wanted to get away from the aching. I actually was expected to deliver a conference paper that day but my voice had completely disappeared with all the screaming I had done. Not being able to complete that task was further debilitating and only reinforced by inability to cope with life's vicissitudes. Something was happening to me. I needed help but did not know where to go.

I wished that I could understand what was happening and why it was causing so much pain in my home. But I was at a loss. There was no reason to feel like this. I just know that I was at my wits end. Plus, there was no one to speak to. My behaviour was damaging to my relationship with my husband and I doubted if other people, my friends or my family could understand objectively what was going on. One night my daughter came into our room because she had a bad dream. She told me that the dream was about me. That I was angry and was about to smash a glass on her head. She said to me, "Mama, I know you would never do that...I just had a bad dream." With that image in my head I knew I needed to get some serious help. I could not bear the thought of my children being afraid of me.

When I first heard of The Bridge, my angel on earth, Mama Eva, had shared with me that a close member of her family who had a history of bipolar mood disorder, had somehow been connected to that place. I didn't know the details but gleaned from her that the place was a source of help and healing. Well I empathised but clearly did not think this was a place for me. I too had misconceptions and misconstrued ideas of what a patient would have to be going through in order to be admitted into a mental hospital. And I did not fit those criteria I had in my head.

I was intrigued about one thing however about this place. It was the fact that they do an intensive, intrusive, comprehensive screening or diagnostic process before entering. With my already established scepticism about being diagnosed as depressed, I was fascinated about a screening process which could tell me more than just that I am clinically depressed, or at the very least, teach me more about what this meant. At the time however, which was about the same time I was first diagnosed, I did not believe that my symptoms warranted a mental hospital, and that surely prayer and seeing a psychologist was sufficient. "I am not crazy" I would think. I do not need to be locked away with others who are talking to invisible people and in strait jackets. Ignorance is a detrimental thing, for apparently I was wrong.

When I had decided that I needed to get help, The Bridge was an option only in the back of my head. I still did not feel I needed that type of help. But my psychologist and medication was not enough. I was still angry and still would engage in uncontrollable fits of rage. And I was desperate.

My psychologist did not think I needed to go there. But my instinct told me I needed something different, something stronger, something that would give me some new answers. And so I woke up that morning on my way to work and ended up taking a deviation that led me to the beginning of my emancipation from this illness.

Popular images of mental hospitals tend to conjure visuals of straitjackets, men and women pacing back and forth in bleach smelling antiseptic white hallways mumbling to themselves, or sporadically yelling random words. The images people hold onto may favour Jack Nicholson's incredible performance in One Flew Over the Cuckoo's Nest. That is, patients in violent rages, or speaking to people who may not be there. But this was not my experience, and oftentimes it is not the typical experience in organizations who give psychiatric treatment to those in need.

If you have cancer you would want to go to an oncologist for treatment. Likewise, if you have a heart problem, you would feel confident in the hands of a cardiologist. Similarly if you have a psychiatric or mental or emotional issue you would want to be in the capable hands of people who are trained in this field and who understand the symptoms, treatment and healing of these types of issues. The Bridge did that for me and more. As I write this book it has only been 2 weeks since I left the hospital, but already I have been given tools and coping mechanisms which should hopefully be instrumental as I apply them in my life. But more than this, my experiences there gave me hope in the face of hopelessness.

Obviously the biblical reference is not about a mental hospital, but it does ask a pertinent question. "Why are you standing out here?" The biblical story refers to a man extending an invitation into his house to a servant who has found in the man's sister a potential wife for his master's son. The servant is considered blessed and stands outside waiting. He is invited in with the question, "Why are you standing out here? I have a room ready for you in my house." Why stand outside of a place that can provide the necessary help you may need when you can walk right in? Why stand outside when there is room available waiting to provide you with shelter and the necessary food for growth. The answer surely lies in the bed of ignorance, lack of knowledge and fear.

Because The Bridge was gnawing away in the back of my head, I had taken the time to attain some knowledge about this facility and what it could possibly do for me. As I had mentioned before the most alluring and inviting aspect of this particular facility was the assessment process before hand. It was also a 24 hour facility so you could walk in at anytime and get that assessment done. I could still hear my angel in the back of my head strongly suggesting for me to go this place because they could help me to understand my self-harming tendencies and they would be thorough in their diagnoses. I still was hesitant however, but steadily growing more curious. The ease with which you could walk in was reminiscent of that question: Why are you standing out there? We have a room ready for you. Just come in, we will take care. I did speak to my husband about the possibility of going to such a facility and he was in full support. If anything, my husband and I may be able to pull back the curtains of not knowing, of being unclear and unsure about what was going on. Still I was not ready but still growing more and more hopeless about my own ability to shift this ubiquitous elephant in the room.

It wasn't until that morning when I was feeling so hopeless, despondent that I decided this was where I needed to go. After leaving my classroom, I drove to the parking lot of the hospital. I sat there and called my husband who was surprised to hear from me as I was supposed to be at work. I told him I was going in and following the assessment I would make a decision or have them make a decision for me about what to do next. I thank God for his calmness and support as I laid this news on him.

As I walked in, I was surprised as to how calm I felt as I said I have come to check myself in. Of course I needed to have the assessment done first. The attendant on duty took me to a small, bare, empty room. As we walked there I looked around each corner waiting to see people in strait jackets rocking themselves to silent lullabies. But I saw no one and did not see anything out of the ordinary. Here I was officially a patient in this institution, officially seeking help and somehow there was a still calmness all around me.

The questions were harrowing as each answer reminded me of the pain and despair I was feeling. I remember needing a lot of tissue and a cigarette even though I don't smoke. At the end of about 30 minutes of an onslaught of questions, the facilitator asked me what I wanted to do. I said I want to be locked away. Locked away I said, from my family, my husband, and my children. I felt I was a source of sadness and pain for them all. I felt I was unworthy and unfit to be around them. I felt like I wanted to disappear. This was safe. While I had been contemplating suicide even on the way over to this hospital, this provided a more secure and protective option. Here was an opportunity to get what I wanted from suicide without killing myself. I can't believe I just wrote that, but that is what I believed.

When I told the female counsellor in front of me in our small quiet room, with its desk and two chairs, that I wanted to be locked away, she nodded emphatically before I could barely get the words out. I was so relieved that she thought the same way. She then said that she would contact the psychiatrist on call and she felt that he would comply with that suggestion. Indeed he did and the next thing I knew, I was being led to what was known as Cottage S*. It is an intensive secure area within the facility for those who need to be stabilized, or those suffering from addictions who are going through detoxification. Nonetheless it was salvation for me. A place I could be safe, I could sleep (for that is what I wanted to do), a place that I could be taken care of. No there were no strait jackets, no antiseptic hallways. Just people who needed help.

Later, my husband brought my clothes and overnight bag. I did not know how long I would be there, but I knew it couldn't be more than 4 days as I had a huge dress rehearsal for a church Easter

---

* Cottage S is a pseudonym for the actual term used at this particular psychiatric facility.

play I wrote for the children. I had to be there, or did I? The time in Cottage S was sacred to me, as I could decompress and embrace the foetal position and seek comfort. But I soon found out it was not a time to slack off or just disengage from the world. It was a time to learn and to focus and to reengage. The time was very structured with periodical medical check ups, specific times for taking medication and many lectures or group therapy sessions to attend. This was a time to learn I felt, about our illness, about coping mechanisms, about our medications and about who we are as valuable, precious people.

I met other patients there who were there for the first time with depression for example who had never considered being in a place like that before. I met people who had depression for the first time after having been considered happy go lucky and extroverted people. I met mothers there struggling with being away from their children. I met wives there who had been brought there by their husbands and loved ones in search for help and at their wits end. I met young men and women with so much potential, so gifted and struggling with depression or other forms of mental illness. This was not a place of "crazy" people talking to invisible demons with straitjackets. This was a hospital like any other hospital with sick people. People with illnesses searching for some help and relief. How wrong I was about psychiatric wellness facilities. This is not to say that people who have schizophrenia do not exist, or that there are no extremes in mental illness. There are. Just like other illnesses where some are more severe than others.

"Why are you standing out there? I have a room ready in my house." I am glad I took up on The Bridge's invitation to come. I am glad I stayed in my Cottage of salvation for three days. I was prepared to at least handle the very exciting very intense dress rehearsal and performance that weekend. On Monday having left Cottage S, it was then time to step down to an intensive Partial Hospitalization program (PHP) which entailed being in their day hospital all day and attending lectures and group therapy sessions. This was where I faced a new opportunity which I found I needed. I call it the cup of tea syndrome.

While I was home for the weekend in-between being discharged from Cottage S and starting the PHP program, I found I still needed to be taken care of. I had no real energy to be giving to others around me, including my family. I was drained and had very little left inside. I found I could not even make a cup of tea for my husband. In a group therapy session, I shared my frustrations and my lack of energy with the group. Anger and resentment was beginning to build inside me because I could not make that darn cup of tea. I resented having to make it, I resented the fact that I had no energy to make it and I resented the fact that I really wanted a cup of tea for myself but just couldn't get one. Obviously my feelings were not about a cup of tea, but rather being overwhelmed, so severely overwhelmed that that cup of tea was almost like the interminable mountain I struggle to climb in my marriage.

After sharing these rather embarrassing feelings, I found such a flood of support coming from individuals in the group. And they were all suggesting I check myself back in to what is known as a halfway house. A place not unlike Cottage S, where there is much security and protection. It is like a dormitory with certain restrictions, but a place where those feelings of being overwhelmed are tremendously cut down and alleviated because of the environment.

The next day I packed a bag ready to be checked into this halfway house. And I stayed there for another six days. While in there, again I met wonderful women who were struggling with their issues trying to get better. I met alcoholics trying to sober up for their families and of course for themselves. I met women with eating disorders, and poor images of themselves trying to love themselves a little bit more. I met women struggling with their weight and overeating, trying to find the source of their food addictions and just simply trying to know and love themselves that much more to get better. I met young women in the prime of their lives, who had damaged their bodies with drugs, and who were making a herculean effort to get back on a healthy path of self-love. Everyday women counted days of sobriety, days of new discoveries, days of joy, days of new beginnings, days of starting over. Every hour in the day was a new opportunity to resist pangs, to fight back negative self-thoughts, to forgive ourselves, to forgive others, to have patience, to be gentle, to forgive ourselves, to love ourselves, to learn new facts, to forgive ourselves, to reach out for help, to meet new people, to share our stories, to forgive ourselves. Again this was not a time to be pampered and to disengage with the world; it was a time to really begin to focus on ourselves, to look within and to take moral inventories of ourselves and our choices in life. If you really want to get better, there is a lot of work a lot of discovery to be done. And one of the places to het help on that journey to discovery is in a mental hospital or mental institution where people are ready and willing to help. It does not mean that you are "crazy" just unwell. It took me a long time to learn that, but I am so glad that I did. I learned so much about myself and about my illness in the bridge.

Chapter 5

"You say Recovery, I say Discovery.":
Healing and Depression

What we see now is like a dim image in a mirror…What I know now is only partial; then it will be complete-as complete as God's knowledge of me. 1 Corinthians13:12

One afternoon while having a group meeting at the halfway house, a young woman was eager to share a story. Phoenix[*] had been at the halfway house for months now and shared how when she had first come she was pretty angry with any concept of a God because she felt God had allowed certain negative things to happen to her. In one of the support groups she attended, another young woman had shared her story of coming to know the Lord. Phoenix said the woman had asked God to prove to her that He existed. She asked him, quite bizarrely, to show her a purple feather if He existed. A few months went by and one day she saw a woman walking with a purple feathered boa around her neck and felt this was close enough. She had become a believer. Well Phoenix was listening eagerly but still quite hesitant to believe in a God. So like the other woman, she did the same and asked God, "If you exist show me a purple feather." We were all intrigued thus far by her story wondering what she had to say about God and a purple feather. Two days later she and

---

[*] All names have been changed.

others were walking to dinner when she noticed a bird's feather on the ground. She stopped and asked one of her friends, "What color is that feather?" She said "It's a purple feather." And there in front of us in our group meeting she pulled out this extraordinarily beautiful and unusual purple feather she picked up off the ground on her way to dinner one evening. That night was the first time she knelt down on her knees and prayed to God.

Discovery. That is what the road to healing is about. Discovery. I tell that story not to say we all have to believe in a God, or am I making any theological statement. I wanted to share that story because of the underlying, titillatilng world of discovery that makes Phoenix's story come alive. This was a brand new discovery for her and that contagious feeling rippled through the common room throughout the souls and hearts of the women listening. That story could mean a new discovery in someone else's life. It is a story of hope, of redemption, of restoration, of healing, of new possibilities. And this is what I am discovering for myself that this journey of healing , this journey towards wholeness is all about.

The buzz word during my time in the halfway house and as a daily patient in the intensive outpatient program on the crossing into healing was "recovery". Recovery is what is understood that the patients are going through. Recovery is the restoration of what was once lost, that is, our health, our confidence, high self esteem perhaps. But while some might say recovery I say discovery. I have felt that during this time, more than anything I am discovering new things about myself, my relationships with other people, and my relationship with myself.

Like Phoenix it is at The Bridge, that I have unearthed new ideas, new ways of believing, and new ways of perceiving the world. It is no coincidence that I have named this psychiatric facility The Bridge. It most certainly acts as a bridge over the river of depression or other mental disorders. On this bridge, we are able to gather necessary coping skills and new knowledge to go forward. To take the next steps. This is not to say that The Bridge, or other places like it, is a guaranteed panacea, rather, it is an opportunity to make some fundamental changes, to engage in deep self –reflection and discover or rediscover aspects of ourselves.

I particularly like the scriptural reference at the beginning of this chapter. It captures so accurately how I feel now having gone through and survived a traumatic depressive episode. "What we see now is like a dim image in a mirror...what I know now is only partial; then it will be complete- as complete as God's knowledge of me." At this time I do not know who I am fully, I am just beginning to discover or re-discover myself. I do see a dim image in the mirror. An image of someone coming into wholeness; becoming clearly visible. I don't see the road to wholeness as an easy one. Honestly, I see it as an opportunity. But we don't always take the opportunities given to us do we? I know that I am on the right path, but I know I will stumble, I will not exercise, or pray, or I'll forget to take my medication. I will probably still feel a little awkward at times talking about depression, but I know that this is the nature of discovery. Like a palaeontologist on a dig, one must be patient and recognize that the big find, the big discovery begins with tiny brushes, sweeping away at the dust. The route to discovery begins with tiny steps.

One of those tiny steps for me was discovering Emotions Anonymous and the Twelve steps that it has at its core on the road to healing. At my first EA meeting I was somewhat nervous and curious about how to proceed. I had never been to anything like that before. When I walked I was first pleasantly surprised to see a multicultural representation of people there. Black, White, Asian; young, old; married and divorced; gay and straight; depressed, bipolar; some more recovered than others, some less; I loved it. Immediately I felt welcomed and understood. After all we were all there for an EA meeting! We were all struggling with some aspect of our emotions. Someone turned down the lights in this small square room. The chairs all lined the perimeter of the room facing inward and we could all look at each other. The obvious leader took her position and began the meeting handing out pamphlets and the like. I noticed some had worn EA books in their hands. There was a routine to it all. Then we went over the Twelve Steps going around the room reading them aloud. As I said before, I was struck and moved by the spiritual approach found in the twelve steps of EA. Some people knew them by heart others followed along in the pamphlets. It felt as if with each reading of a Step, the spiritual level in the room rose. The leader then read a daily meditation and we went around the room sharing our stories that may or may not be connected to that reading. Tears fell. Truths abounded. People laughed together. People cried together. There was respect in the room. Some opted to pass on their turn. Some shared their challenges with following and adhering to the Steps. It was beautiful.

The Steps, I have discovered, are comprehensive and follow a logical and natural path. Without knowing these steps even existed, they were happening to me, or I was doing them at least the first few of them. But it is when we are deliberate about accomplishing these Steps, is when the real change occurs and when true discovery happens. The first Step is to admit we are powerless over our emotions that our life has become unmanageable. But admit to whom? To me yes, this occurred with time and reflection especially after seeing a psychologist and psychiatrist. Taking the time to reflect or have someone hold up an emotional mirror in front of you, is needed to accomplish this first step in the 12 step process towards a more content and manageable life. Mama Eva was my saviour at this point, my reflector. It was liberating to admit my helplessness to her. And then to have that admission met with support, love, good advice and new direction, was more than I could ask for. But know that my going to seek help at the Bridge came about *two years* after she first told me about it. I never said discovery was easy or quick!

The next two steps are about admitting our powerlessness to God or to a Power greater than ourselves, which will restore us to sanity and making a decision to turn our will and our lives over to the care of God *as we understood Him.* Again letting go and letting God. For a long time I was unable to even pray to God much less hand over my powerlessness to Him. I am just getting to that point now. But there is another dimension to this which only became clear to me while reading The Language of Letting Go. One has to be ready for the blessings. Asking for blessings is one thing but being ready to receive that inheritance is another. In the daily meditation book Beattie says, "Do not ask for love unless you're ready to be healed enough to give and receive love. Do not ask for joy unless you're ready to feel and release your pain so you can feel joy. Do not ask for success unless you're ready to conquer the behaviors that would sabotage success. Today God give me the courage to identify the good I want in my life and to ask for it. Give me also the faith and stamina I need to go through the work that must be accomplished first."

Am I ready to enjoy the love that I so crave? Am I ready to love myself? What about others? Am I ready to give that love to my children, my husband, my family? During the depths of my depression I used to wonder whether or not I loved my children, or whether they loved me. I can't believe I just admitted that. I used to cringe when my husband told me he loved me. How could he possibly love me? I would ask myself. What is there to love? I want to give love back but it is so far out of my reach, so deep inside me covered by all the self-hate and negative thoughts, I couldn't reach it. What about success? I used to be afraid of success, which was some twisted fear of failure. I was afraid of doing well, even as far back as high school exams. So sometimes, without even knowing it I found myself sabotaging the successes that were in my reach. Are you ready for your blessing? Are you ready for your inheritance?

Steps four and five are about peeling back the lens of denial and first making a searching and fearless moral inventory of ourselves. And I feel the key word there is fearless. You can't be afraid of what you're going to find out about yourself when you engage in the moral inventory. Then after making this moral inventory, admitting to God, to ourselves and to another human being the exact nature of our wrongs. This is probably one of the most difficult things to do because not only do we have to claim our own shortcomings but then we have to admit them to another human being. Once again the concept of bringing people into the discovery process is integral. Step 6 ironically enough is about being entirely ready to have God remove all the defects of character we may have found within ourselves. This is a blessing in and of itself, recognizing the defects of character and being ready to have God remove them.

The next two steps involve not only admitting to other people but making direct amends with those who you have harmed or hurt or disappointed through your emotional struggle. One of the most liberating moments for me during my route to wholeness was in the Bridge, when my husband had to come in and meet with myself and a counsellor. It was simply a gift from God to be able to tell my husband in no uncertain terms, I am sick, I am depressed, and I am so sorry for anything I have done to ever hurt you or cause you pain in any way. My children are a more delicate situation, but I am just beginning to "know" them again. Any time my children say that they love me, my heart flips over, my throat closes up and the tears well up in my eyes. It is a precious thing to know that you are loved but even more treasured to receive it unencumbered. It is as if I am piecing together that dim image in the mirror. Putting parts of me I used to know, parts of me I wanted to know and new parts I have discovered, together to form the child of God I should know I am. After all He knew us from in the womb, He formed us and formed our entire lives. And that brings us back to the eleventh step which is about praying only for knowledge of His will for us and the power to carry that out.

Not too long ago I got a tattoo of the fleur de lis on my ankle. I chose that image after I read in an old church book that it was used to symbolise Mary, the mother of Jesus. At the time, I thought that was perfect because Mary had become a "she-ro" of mine. She ultimately embodied what I felt a thirty-something wife and mother should be. Even though she was a teenager, she took life's challenges with a sophistication and maturity that I could only hope to have. When faced with the news of becoming an unwed teenage mother, she simply said, "Let it be according to thy will." If only I could have faced marriage, children life's struggles, my depression like that I feel I would be a better woman for it.

The final step brings all this work together in what they term a spiritual awakening. Having had a spiritual awakening as a result of these steps, the mission is then to carry the message and principles in all of life's affairs. These steps are not just about depression for me but about a new approach, a new way of seeing the world and my role in it. It is a world of new discoveries! But I also recognize that these steps are meaningless without being bathed in faith.

Jesus said to Thomas "Do you believe because you see me? How happy are those who believe without seeing me." What he was talking about here was faith. And I have found that faith is an integral part of this journey towards discovery. Faith is what sustains us, what helps us to keep going, to keep trying. I don't want to end this book, having you believe that I now have got it together. That would be ludicrous! It is only the beginning but I feel fortunate to have learned some pretty powerful things along the way and I wanted to share them with you. It is a lifelong journey not something I can possibly attain tomorrow but I can get clearer about as I go forward.

As for now, I am a thirty-something woman, Christian, mother, wife, battling depression, survivor of depression; grateful; determined to be a better me; committed to change; faithful; trying to read the bible more; hoping to be a better lover of life, of love, of myself, of my husband, of my family; lover of dance; lover of music; trying to exercise more for my health's sake; lover of God; seeking to be a better prayer warrior; unafraid; not embarrassed; patient; humble; seeking to be free; seeking to be more positive; seeking to love myself; hoping to love myself; praying to love myself; just trying to make it to the next day, to see a new morning.

Afterword

"Me? Still Depressed?":
Relapse and Depression

I write this a year later in the common room at the Bridge. I checked myself back in following a crisis episode...Following a night in which I realized that well, all things were not right in the universe! I ran head on into a situation in which I did not use the coping mechanisms and skills and insight I had learned to rely on in the hospital a year ago. I did not stop to pray, I did not stop to consider what I could use to help me.

After I left the hospital a year ago, when I first checked myself in, I felt so ready to face my life again with new tools. I was energized. I found a psychologist. I continued to take my medication. I was exercising every day. And I even had rediscovered some of what used to bring me joy. I started to write again. Like I shared before, I went to Jamaica to recuperate following my initial stay in the hospital. There I promised myself I would exercise every day, write diligently everyday and focus on healing away from my family. At first I felt like I was abandoning my family by going away from them for two weeks, but deep down I knew I needed to be away from them, to re-strengthen so that I could face them again anew, renewed and fortified.

In Jamaica I focused on rediscovering myself, but most importantly it was a therapeutic time as I sat down to write down my experiences. Each word seemed to act as glue piecing back together what had fallen apart during my depressive episode. Looking back at the mental hospital, at the people I met there, at the discoveries I made there, helped to bring m body and my mind towards wholeness. I felt I was on the right track. Then that night came, about a year later, where I completely lost control.

The emotions of that night were brewing for days before. I just didn't realise it. I had been on a second medical leave from work for a few months and my writing had been fully revived. I was writing everyday and getting further and further into the story I was creating, perhaps to the detriment of those around me. Nonetheless, I was beginning to feel my world falling out of balance. When that happens, little things around me begin to bother me and if I am not careful, I could just implode. I take things so personally when I am in that mode. I began to question whether I was spending too much time writing, something from which I gained much pleasure. I was feeling guilty and soon started down that slippery slope of feeling like a failure, like I was not being a good mother and wife. Before long, the old familiar feelings of lack of self-worth, low self-esteem, low self-image came flooding back to drown me. Nothing of what I had learned in the hospital could stop me from going down this route. It was too late. A deluge of tears washed in with the old feelings. The anger resurfaced again in a violent rage and the easiest solution I could think of was ending my life right then and there. That way the kids would not have to deal with a selfish mother or my husband with a withdrawn wife. When I feel at my lowest these suicidal thoughts are a comfort and ultimately feel like the only way out.   Realising the danger of these thoughts, I remembered the place to go where I would be safe and my children and husband would be safe. So I got in the car and drove myself to the place which saved my life once before, the Bridge.

I got there at about 1am, got checked in and had to sleep out in the common room under suicide watch. It was late, it was cold and uncomfortable in the leather foldout beds they have in the common room. Yet somehow, I felt out of harm's way, protected and calm. Here I was again! Although I was relaxed and grateful to be there, I felt like more of a failure for ending back up in this place, to which I was sure, I would not return. The next morning I awoke to a new yet familiar regimen of lectures and group therapy sessions. And again as people shared their stories and voiced their lives, I realised we were all just sick, looking for some help. I met new people with similar stories; new men and women, young and old, black and white, all who were there seeking help. As I sat in the groups among these broken people, I made a startling new discovery.

I learned a new word....relapse. I had only thought of that word in the context of alcoholism or people who use drugs. But I indeed had a relapse of depression. It happened again. I was feeling overwhelmed, out of control, the tears were falling incessantly, I felt I had nowhere to turn and at the bottom of all of that, there was the constant thought of suicide as the only way out. As the only reprieve. That is, until I thought of checking myself back in at the Bridge and getting the help I so desperately needed.

"Me? Depressed?"

You see, this Afterword is important because it is not unfathomable to have bouts of depression. This may be a no brainer to many of you but it was not for me. I thought that with the tools I learned at the Bridge, the medication I was taking and the consistent visits with a psychologist and psychiatrist; the prayer and meditation; and with the support of my family, I would be fine. However that was not the case and I had a relapse. A relapse I am learning now is simply a normal part of the process, the journey towards recovery, or discovery as I call it. And it is not necessarily my fault.

When I speak to my current psychologist he often refers to the overarching umbrella of my recovery, "Beth's Recovery" he calls it. It is a large umbrella which encompasses every action I take and every decision I make. He often questions whether or not a particular action or decision is helpful under the overall umbrella of "Beth's recovery". And I am learning now, it is becoming second nature to question that for myself each time I think about taking a step in a new direction. "Is this really good for my recovery?" "What can I do to make it better for my recovery?" "I know that this is not at all going to be good for my overall recovery!!!" At times it becomes somewhat of a game!

But in retrospect I can now look soberly at what I was doing or not doing since my first hospital stay which led to my crisis episode and my consequent relapse. Believe me, these things are easily done. What I had to work through was the guilt and shame about having a relapse.

When I first left the hospital as I said in the final chapter, I was a thirty something woman, wife, mother; trying to be a healthier person; trying to pray more, laugh more, talk more, share more, give more; I was basically trying to get my feet back under me so that I could begin to walk again and rejoin the journey of my life. So I stepped out and found a new psychologist, someone to talk to and walk with on the journey to recovery. I began to change some of my old ways of being, letting go of my negative self-talk and building up my low self-esteem. I was so committed to getting better! And being better in the eyes of those around me. My husband, my children, my colleagues from work. I so wanted to be done with this crutch called depression. All my energy was directed towards doing the things necessary to heal myself and fix what I had made a mess of at home and at work.

With my new psychologist I focused on ways to organize my life so that I could have more control over the daily vicissitudes of life. He became more of a life coach than a psychologist. I was not so focused on addressing my psychological needs as I was fixing the world around me. I figured that if everything around me was straight I would automatically be too. So I bought a push board and a white board for the kitchen. I wrote down everything the kids did and when they did it. I made a calendar for our lives. Because organization can counteract crazy! I tried to be more communicative with my husband and give of myself more. To be present in our marriage. I continued to share with my angel on earth my journey and had prayer sessions. I took my medicine everyday and made sure I did not lapse on that. And I was exercising every day. Trying to do something to get the blood flowing and my heart pumping.

Because I had left my workplace suddenly and during the semester, I had papers to grade. I organized myself as much as I could to mark the ninety plus papers I had to grade. Things were changing. At least it felt like my life was changing.

I was doing all the right things. From the perspective of the Bridge I was accomplishing all the necessary tools- eating right and exercise, seeing a psychologist, seeing a psychiatrist, taking my meds—all except for joining a support group. And I thought I was getting that support through the psychologist. I was wrong. Nonetheless I pushed forward. Soon the Fall semester was back in session and I was off to a good start at work. With juggling work, family and my health, the bottom soon fell out. I was totally overwhelmed and didn't even know it. I was not ready to go back to work. Going back so soon was not good for "Beth's Recovery" but I could not see it. I wanted to prove to others and to myself that I was capable. Not of anything in particular, just capable. Because when I realised I was battling clinical depression I felt like a complete failure.

I noticed at work, I was beginning to wear the mask again. I was one way on the exterior: pleasant, capable and productive. And one way on the interior: scared, overwhelmed and unbalanced. One evening while on a conference call with the rest of my team, I could not participate in the way I felt I needed to, got off the phone and decided I could not go back. I simply could not go back. Three days later I was on another medical leave of absence and a few months later found myself late at night on my way back to the Bridge.

You can have the best intentions, but somehow you are not able to heal as quickly as you would like. Much like maintaining one's sobriety, it is a constant effort, a day to day endeavour to live with clinical depression. It is so easy to lapse back into negative self-thinking, into low self-esteem, into questioning one's worth and value. It is so easy to convince oneself that suicide is the best way out of a situation. It is so easy.

But of course, you know where I'm going with this. No matter how easy it is to fall back into these destructive ways of thinking, it is not worth it for the overall health of the recovery umbrella. The recovery umbrella becomes the most significant part of your healing. Every action has to be thought of in terms of the health of the recovery umbrella. I really have to thank my current therapist for that precious gem. It is simple but so poignant in the road to full recovery.

Depression is a serious medical condition that does not discriminate. I pray that if you or someone you know battles depression, that you will first realise that fact. Then I pray for you the understanding that depression is not a failure and it is not your fault. I want you to know that you can get help, whether you use medication or not. Help is out there in all forms; please open your eyes to see them. Close your eyes to the stereotypes and stigmas. Love yourself. Love yourself. Love yourself. Realise that there is power in prayer. Especially in the serenity prayer which I discovered is often used at the end of Emotions Anonymous meetings and in the world of mental illness. God, grant me the serenity to accept the things I cannot change, the courage to change the things I can and the wisdom to know the difference. God is so good that God wants you to be well, spiritually, physically and mentally.

I still am a thirty something woman, wife, mother, Christian, believer; thanking God for each day; realizing that my life is worth it (at least most of the time); taking my meds; trying to believe in myself a bit more; learning to love my children more; learning to love my husband more; learning to love myself more; exercising everyday (or when I have enough energy to do it); trying to eat right; trying to be more present to my family; getting to know my children better; enjoying them more and more each day; trying to get enough sleep; doing what I enjoy the most (now that I've re-discovered those things); trying to read the bible more (when I have the energy to do that); forgiving myself; not blaming myself; trying to forget more; trying to remember who I am; who I used to be.

---

[i] Radulovacki, Branko, "The Basics of Mental Illness" Ridgeview Institute.

[ii] Copeland, Mary Ellen, "Living without depression & Manic Depression"

[iii] Ibid.

[iv] Radulovacki, Branko, "The Basics of Mental Illness" Ridgeview Institute

[v] Ibid.

[vi] Ibid.

[vii] Webster's New World Dictionary of the American Language

[viii] The Book of Common Prayer, p. 134.

[ix] Colquhoun, Frank (Ed.) Parish Prayers, Hodder and Stoughton: London, 1971, p. 302.

www.ingramcontent.com/pod-product-compliance
Lightning Source LLC
Chambersburg PA
CBHW031219270326
41931CB00006B/613